ANIMALS AT WORK

Animals
Surviving in Extreme
Environments

WORLD
BOOK

World Book, Inc.
180 North LaSalle Street
Suite 900
Chicago, Illinois 60601
USA

Produced for World Book, Inc. by Bailey Publishing Associates Ltd.

For information about other World Book publications, visit our website at **www.worldbook.com** or call **1-800-WORLDBK (967-5325)**.

Library of Congress Cataloging-in-Publication data has been applied for.

Title: Animals Surviving in Extreme Environments
ISBN: 978-0-7166-2736-4

Animals at Work
ISBN: 978-0-7166-2724-1 (set, hc)

Also available as:
ISBN: 978-0-7166-2749-4 (e-book)

Printed in China by Shenzhen Wing King Tong
Paper Products Co, Ltd., Shenzhen, Guangdong
1st printing August 2018

4338

Staff

Writer: Alex Woolf

Executive Committee

President
Jim O'Rourke

Vice President and Editor in Chief
Paul A. Kobasa

Vice President, Finance
Donald D. Keller

Vice President, Marketing
Jean Lin

Vice President, International
Maksim Rutenberg

Vice President, Technology
Jason Dole

Director, Human Resources
Bev Ecker

Editorial

Director, Print Publishing
Tom Evans

Managing Editor
Jeff De La Rosa

Editor
William D. Adams

Manager, Contracts & Compliance
(Rights & Permissions)
Loranne K. Shields

Manager, Indexing Services
David Pofelski

Librarian
S. Thomas Richardson

Digital

Director, Digital Product
Development
Erika Meller

Digital Product Manager
Jonathan Wills

Manufacturing/Production

Manufacturing Manager
Anne Fritzinger

Proofreader
Nathalie Strassheim

Graphics and Design

Senior Art Director
Tom Evans

Senior Designer
Don Di Sante

Media Editor
Rosalia Bledsoe

Special thanks to:

Roberta Bailey
Nicola Barber
Francis Paola Lea
Claire Munday
Alex Woolf

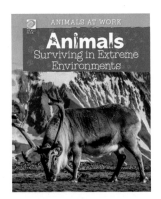

A reindeer grazes in Svalbard, a group of islands midway between Norway and the North Pole. Reindeer live in the extreme cold of northern Europe and Asia.

Acknowledgments

Cover photo: © Incredible Arctic/Shutterstock

Alamy: 5 (Cindy Hopkins), 7 (Alvin Chan), 10-11, 12, 27 & 29 (Minden Pictures), 12-13 (Robert Harding), 15 (WILDLIFE GmbH), 16 (Norman Owen Tomalin), 18 (Cultura RM), 19 (Ann and Steve Toon), 21 (Zoltan Molnar), 22-23 (Chris Mattison), 24-25 (Stephen Frink Collection), 25 (Newscom), 26-27 (Solvin Zankl), 28 & 38-39 (Paulo Oliveira), 28-29 (Nature Picture Library), 31 (Science History Images), 37 & 39 (SuperStock), 41 (blickwinkel), 42 (Ivan Kuzmin). **J. Bedek**: 42-43. **Hectonichus**: 44-45. **Shutterstock**: title & 18-19 (Bildagentur Zoonar GmbH), 4 (PYP), 6-7 (Giedriius), 9 (Roger Clark ARPS), 10 (Sophia Granchinho), 13 (Jukka Jantunen), 14 (A. J. Gallant), 14-15 (FloridaStock), 16-17 (Vaclav Sebek), 17 (Paul Prescot), 20 (vblinov), 20-21 (Michael Potter11), 22 (Kambiz Pourghanad), 23 (fivespots), 32-33 (Marina Poushkina), 33 (David Havel), 34-35 (Yongyut Kumsri), 35 (thatmacroguy). **US Fish & Wildlife Service**: 43 (Gordon Smith). **Yerpo**: 45.

Contents

Introduction

People live all over the world. They live mostly in places that are not too hot and not too cold, and neither too wet nor too dry. People can live in tough environments by wearing special clothes, building special structures, or even changing their behavior, such as when they choose to go outside. Like people, most animals can be found in places where there is a good climate and lots of food. But some **species** have also found ways of surviving in less comfortable places. In fact, some animals live in places that we humans need special equipment to visit even for a short time.

Animals live in many extreme environments. Polar bears, musk oxen, and penguins can withstand the freezing conditions near the North and South poles. And the world's hot, dry deserts are home to many different species, including camels, lizards, **rodents,** foxes, and frogs. Such animals as the snow leopard and the Himalayan jumping spider can withstand the thin air of the highest mountain peaks.

The jumping spider has excellent vision with four big eyes facing forward and four smaller eyes on top of its head.

Beneath Earth's surface, species of fish, **insects,** and **amphibians** have managed to live in the constant darkness of underground caves. But perhaps most strange and surprising are the creatures that live in the deepest oceans, such as the blobfish and the giant tubeworm. While conditions may be tough in these environments, there is also usually less competition for resources and fewer **predators.** So those animals that can live in these **habitats** do well.

In this book, you will read about some of the different kinds of animals that live in extreme environments. You will learn how their bodies are different from those of animals living in less extreme climates, and what sorts of behaviors help them survive.

Sky survivors

Some spiderlings (young spiders) purposely set out on dangerous—even deadly—journeys. They make threads of silk, pushing the threads out of their bodies to catch the wind and take them on rides through the sky that can go high into the upper atmosphere. By this process, called ballooning, they can travel hundreds of miles or kilometers, often surviving weeks without food. Though many of them die, some spiderlings live to spread to new places, such as islands and mountaintops.

The central netted dragon is a type of lizard found in sandy deserts of Australia. It digs burrows to avoid the extreme heat of the desert.

Life in the Cold

The Arctic (the area surrounding the North Pole) and the Antarctic (the area surrounding the South Pole) are extremely cold places. But some animals manage to live in these polar climates.

PHYSICAL ADAPTATIONS

Many **mammals** that live in polar areas grow fur for insulation, trapping a layer of air close to the skin. The musk ox, which lives in the Arctic, has two coats to protect it during the freezing winter. Its outer coat is made up of long, shaggy hairs, known as guard hairs. These cover a shorter, very warm undercoat. When spring comes, the musk ox sheds its undercoat.

FROZEN FROGS

Amphibians are **cold-blooded,** meaning that they use outside sources of heat, usually the sun, to warm their bodies. Because of this, few amphibians live in cooler climates, let alone in the Arctic. But the North American wood frog can survive as far north as the U.S. state of Alaska and northern Canada, thanks to its remarkable ability to freeze and then thaw. The wood frog lives for weeks or months in a state of **hibernation,** with two-thirds of its body's water frozen. The frog stops breathing and its heart stops beating. Usually, animals' cells are harmed or killed by the process of freezing and thawing. But the wood frog's body contains substances that lower the freezing point of its **tissues.** This limits the amount of ice that forms in the frog's cells and allows it to survive.

Fat and fur

Polar bears have a dense (thick), insulating undercoat covered with guard hairs. Their skin is black, so they can hold as much heat as possible from the sun. Beneath their skin lies a layer of fat that can measure up to 4.5 inches (11.5 centimeters) thick. This fat layer keeps the polar bears warm when they swim. Their fur is oily, so it does not soak up the cold water. Polar bears also have small, round ears and short tails, limiting the amount of heat that is lost through these parts of their bodies.

A polar bear swims in the Arctic waters off the coast of Norway.

A musk ox in winter. The hairs of the musk ox's undercoat can be used to make a very soft, warm wool called qiviut (KIH vee uht).

The Emperor Penguin

The emperor penguin is the only animal to live on the open ice of Antarctica during the winter. It endures wind chills as cold as -76 °F (-60 °C) and blizzards with winds of up to 125 miles (200 kilometers) per hour. Its body has developed in ways to help it survive such extreme weather.

The emperor penguin is big—the largest of all the penguins at around 45 inches (115 centimeters) tall—allowing it to hold more heat. An animal loses heat to the outside world through its skin, which covers the outer surface of its body. The larger an animal is, the less surface area it has compared to its size. Because of this, larger animals, such as the emperor penguin, can better survive in extreme cold. An emperor penguin also has a small beak and flippers, keeping its surface area as small as possible.

The emperor penguin has special areas in its beak that catch most of the heat from its breath. Its short, stiff tail forms a tripod with its heels to reduce contact with the ice. Its feet have special fats that keep them from freezing and strong claws to grip the ice.

The emperor penguin has several layers of scalelike feathers that protect it from the cold and give it a waterproof coat. It has muscles that can raise and lower these feathers. The penguin raises them when on land, forming an insulating layer of air next to its skin. When swimming, the penguin flattens down its feathers to reduce **drag** and contact between its skin and the icy water. Beneath the feathers is a layer of fat that insulates its body and serves as an energy source.

The emperor penguin also behaves in ways to help it deal with the harsh environment. The penguins huddle together in large groups to protect themselves from the wind and keep warm. Individual penguins take turns moving between the warmer center of the group and the chilly outside.

An EMPEROR PENGUIN with three chicks. The chicks are covered with soft down which keeps them warm on land, but not in water. The chicks must molt and grow new feathers before they can swim.

BEHAVIORAL ADAPTATIONS

Animals living near the poles need to stay warm and find food if they are to survive the long winter. As well as physical adaptations, they also have special ways of behaving that help them to cope with the cold.

Some animals get through the winter by **hibernating.** During hibernation, the animal's body temperature goes down, and its heart rate and breathing slow. The Arctic ground squirrel, which lives in the North American Arctic **tundra,** hibernates for seven months every year. It lives in burrows, which it digs in sandy soil on mountain slopes, riverbanks, and ridges. In late summer, it begins to store food in its burrow, so it has something to eat when it wakes in the spring. In the fall, it eats plants, seeds, and fruit to build up its body fat, almost doubling its weight before winter hibernation. It makes its burrow warmer by lining it with insulating material, such as musk ox hair, leaves, and lichen (*LY kuhn).*

The lemming is a small **rodent** that also lives in the North American tundra. During winter the lemming lives in burrows in the ground insulated with leaves and grasses. Unlike the Arctic ground squirrel, the lemming does not hibernate. It stays active throughout the winter, finding food by digging into the snow to reach plants and **insects,** or by eating grasses it stored earlier. Due to the warmth of its burrow, lemmings can breed (make more animals like themselves) and care for and feed young in the winter.

The Arctic hare does not hibernate, but survives the winter by digging shelters in the ground or under the snow to keep warm and sleep. Although they normally live alone, Arctic hares sometimes gather in large groups and huddle together in snow shelters for warmth during the winter months.

The Arctic hare is well adapted to life on the Arctic tundra.

Bears: super sleepers

Many bears spend the cold months in a state called winter sleep. This is not real hibernation. Like true hibernators, their heart rate and breathing slows. But their body temperature does not drop much. Due to their large size (see page 8) and layers of fur and fat, they can keep themselves warm all winter even with their **metabolism** (*muh TAB uh lihz uhm*) slowed to less than half of its normal rate. Because they stay warm during their sleep, they can wake up quickly to respond to danger outside their den. True hibernators need many hours to warm themselves up before they can become fully active again. Most true hibernators must also stop hibernating every few days to eat and drink or urinate and defecate (*YUR uh nayt, DEHF uh kayt;* release solid and liquid wastes), and even to sleep! But a bear does not need to eat, drink, urinate, or defecate during its winter sleep.

An Arctic ground squirrel hibernates in its burrow.

DEALING WITH SNOW AND ICE

Snow can be deep and hard to wade through. Ice is slippery. Animals living near the poles have different ways of dealing with the challenges of snow and ice. Penguins, for example, will sometimes lie on their stomachs and slide across an icy surface, using their flippers to brake and steer. This "tobogganing" method is often faster than walking and can use less energy.

Polar bears have large paws up to 12 inches (30 centimeters) wide. These help spread out the bear's weight across thin ice, lessening the chance of it breaking. The bears' grip is further improved by thick black pads on the soles of their feet, which are covered in tiny bumps. These bumps create friction between foot and ice, keeping the bears from slipping.

Caribou (*KAR uh boo*) migrate long distances to find food during the Arctic winter. Their feet are well adapted for journeys across deep snow, frozen lakes, and soggy ground. Their large hooves have four toes. The two rear toes, called dewclaws, are small. The two front toes are big, crescent-shaped, and support most of the animal's weight. The underside of a caribou hoof is hollow, and the animal can use it like a shovel to dig through snow in search of mosses or grass to eat. The hoof's sharp edges also give the caribou extra grip on rocks or ice.

Caribou hooves are good at gripping icy surfaces.

Adélie penguins "toboggan" towards the sea at Brown Bluff, Antarctica.

Camouflage

Some Arctic animals use the snow itself as **camouflage.** As winter approaches, they shed their summer coats and grow white fur to make themselves harder to see against the snowy background. This can help them hide from **predators,** or to sneak up on **prey.** Examples include the Arctic fox, the Arctic hare, and the stoat—often called the ermine when in its white winter coat.

An ermine in its white winter fur in Yukon, Canada.

GLOBAL WARMING

Since the mid-1900's, Earth's average surface temperature has been rising. This is known as **global warming.** Scientists have found strong evidence that human activities, such as the burning of fossil fuels, are a major cause. The warming is already affecting the poles and the animals that live near and on them. The impacts are likely to get worse as time goes on.

Temperatures in the Arctic are rising more than twice as fast as the global average, and sea ice is shrinking by nearly four percent per decade. Polar bears use sea ice as a platform for hunting seals. In all areas of the Arctic, polar bears have already experienced some loss of sea ice. With the ice retreating earlier in spring and forming later in winter, polar bears have less time to hunt **prey** and must go without food for longer.

In Alaska, a warmer, drier climate will probably cause forests to grow into areas of meadow, bog, and fen, reducing the **habitat** of such **species** as caribou, beaver, otter, fox, and waterfowl. Beavers build dams, which help create and protect wetlands. A reduction in beaver numbers will speed up the loss of wetlands and all the species that depend on them.

A beaver dam. These dams help protect wetland areas.

Antarctic krill

Small **crustaceans** called krill are an important part of the Antartic **ecosystem.** Krill hatch in the cold waters around Antarctica. During the winter, they take shelter under sea ice and eat the **algae** that grows there. As the planet warms, less sea ice will form, leaving less space for krill to grow. As their numbers decline, the populations of the many animals that eat them, such as whales, seals, and penguins, will suffer, too.

Antarctic krill is the main food of baleen whales.

A polar bear and her cub walk on an ice floe in the Norwegian Arctic. Polar bears do most of their hunting in the spring when ringed seal pups appear. The early melting of sea ice is making it harder for them to feed during this important time.

Desert Animals

Desert animals are adapted to live in a dry and hot world. They must deal with little water, extreme heat, and burning, slippery sand.

SAVING WATER

Animals need water for their bodies to function, but they can lose it through breathing, sweating, and urinating and defecating. Because there is so little rainfall in the desert, the bodies of animals that live there are designed to limit the water they lose through these physical processes.

The kangaroo rat, a **rodent** of the deserts of North and Central America, does not have sweat **glands,** so it loses little water through its skin. Its feces (*FEE seez;* solid wastes) are five times drier than those of a laboratory rat. Its kidneys remove most of the water from its urine and return it to its bloodstream. When the kangaroo rat breathes, **organs** in its nose take out much of the moisture in the air it exhales and return it to the body.

The kangaroo rat has an oily coat that helps it to hold in moisture.

Desert birds, such as the Arabian waxbill, have oils on their skin that reduce evaporation (the changing from a liquid to a gas) of moisture. The Gila (*HEE luh*) monster, a large lizard, stores water in fat in its tail. The water-holding frog of Australia stores water in its bladder as well as in pockets in its skin. It can take the water back into its **tissues** when it needs to.

Camels

Camels are very well adapted to their desert **habitat.** They lose little moisture through physical functions. When they eat, their thick lips can grasp leaves without losing moisture from their tongues. Their nostrils can trap water vapor from their breath and return it to their bodies. Their feces are very dry, and they urinate less than most **mammals.** They sweat little, and when they do, it evaporates on their skin beneath their fur to aid cooling. The camel stores fat in its hump, which it breaks down into water and energy when none can be found in its environment.

Camels drink when they can, and may travel up to 100 miles (160 kilometers) without water.

The Gila monster is the largest lizard in the United States.

GETTING WATER

Water is very hard to find in the desert. Many desert animals can survive without drinking at all. Instead, they get all the moisture they need from their food. Kit foxes get their water from the flesh of **rodents,** rabbits, and other **prey.** Elf owls get enough water from eating **insects** and scorpions. Many desert insects get water by taking nectar or sap from plants, or by eating leaves and fruit. Other animals, such as coyotes, mule deer, and bighorn sheep, need to drink once in a while, so they can never stray too far from a water hole.

The thorny devil, a lizard of the Australian desert, has an unusual way of collecting water. It cannot lick water from puddles because its mouth has **evolved** to eat only ants. Instead, the creature finds a patch of damp sand and stands on it. Narrow grooves in its skin suck up the moisture in the sand by a process called capillary action. The grooves funnel the water toward the creature's mouth. The lizard then squeezes the water inside its mouth in tiny gulps. If it cannot get enough moisture this way, the thorny devil will bury itself in the damp sand to drink. Another method is to wait for droplets of dew to collect on its skin during the night. It then channels this water to its mouth.

An elf owl in its cactus house in the southwestern U.S. state of Arizona.

Harvesting water from fog

The darkling beetle lives in the Namib Desert of southern Africa, one of the driest places on Earth. It gets the water it needs from fog that comes in off the ocean, which it collects on its back. The beetle stands on a ridge of sand, facing the ocean, and raises its **abdomen** into the air. This is known as the fog-basking stance. The beetle's hard wing cases are covered in tiny bumps, which attract water. Tiny droplets of moisture in the fog collect on these bumps. When the droplets get too heavy to stick to the bumps, they roll down the beetle's back to its mouth.

A darkling beetle collects water from the fog in the Namib Desert.

Water flows to the thorny devil's mouth through narrow grooves in its skin.

DEALING WITH HEAT

Desert animals usually move about at dawn, dusk, or at night to avoid the heat of the day. **Insects, rodents,** toads, lizards, and tortoises shelter in underground burrows or cracks in rocks or the ground during the hottest periods. Birds, such as the prairie falcon, nest on ledges on north-facing cliffs to avoid direct sunlight.

Some animals, such as frogs and turtles, escape the heat for months at a time by **estivating**—going into an inactive state like **hibernation**—in burrows. The water-holding frog (see page 16) covers itself in **mucus** and buries itself underground during long dry periods, only waking when the rains return.

Desert sheep, goats, donkeys, and camels have areas on their legs and bellies with little fur, which help them give off heat. Birds can lose heat through their featherless legs in the same way. They can also pant (breathe quickly) to cool down. Jack rabbits have long legs that keep most of their body clear of the hot ground. Their long ears are full of blood vessels that help pass body heat into the air.

The addax antelope has a white summer coat that reflects the sun's heat rather than taking it in.

Desert animals find shade wherever they can. Birds called cactus wrens rest in the shadow of yucca plants. Pallid bats spend their days sleeping in cracks along cliff faces. The pack rat builds itself a den of sticks, stones, and cactus pieces. The Cape ground squirrel, a rodent of the desert areas of southern Africa, uses its bushy tail as a kind of portable shade.

Fennec foxes

The fennec fox, which lives in the Sahara, the world's largest desert, is well adapted to the hot, arid climate. Its large ears, which measure up to 6 inches (15 centimeters) in length, contain many blood vessels close to the skin, helping to give off heat. As well as keeping it cool, its ears are extremely sensitive, allowing it to sense **prey** and avoid **predators.**

The fennec fox has the largest ears of any fox compared to its body size.

The Cape ground squirrel uses its tail to protect itself from the hot sun.

A WORLD OF SAND

Apart from heat and dryness, sand is a major feature of many deserts. Sand is hard to walk on and can get extremely hot. When the wind blows, sand gets into animals' eyes, ears, and nostrils. Desert **species** have adapted to sand in different ways. Some even use it to their advantage.

Addax antelopes, camels, and kangaroo rats have broad, flat hooves or feet to support their weight on the shifting sand grains, helping them walk without sinking. The fennec fox and the sand cat have fur on the soles of their feet to protect them from the hot sand. The sidewinder, a snake of the southwestern United States, moves in a wavelike pattern that helps give it traction on loose desert sands, and also keeps it from touching the hot surface too long at a time.

A camel's long eyelashes and hair-covered ears help keep sand out of its eyes and ears. Its nostrils can close to keep sand from blowing into its nose. Meerkats can close their ears to keep sand out, and have a third eyelid to protect their eyes.

The camel's ears and eyes are adapted to its desert environment.

Some desert animals have adapted to life under the sand. The fringe-toed lizard of the western U.S. state of California can burrow quickly beneath the sand to avoid **predators.** Special scales keep sand out of its ears, and its nostrils are adapted to help it breathe under the sand. The golden mole of the Namib Desert lives the whole day underground, using its powerful legs and pointy snout to "swim" through the sand. In a world without light, the mole is blind, but has a good sense of hearing. Vibrations in the sand grains carry the sounds of its **insect prey.**

Kenyan sand boa

The Kenyan sand boa is a burrowing desert snake of East Africa that eats small **mammals.** It spends most of its life in a shallow burrow beneath the sand with only its head out, waiting for its prey to approach. The snake then rears up and grabs its victim. Sometimes it will drag the prey under the sand to suffocate it.

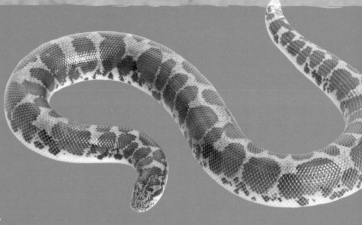

The Kenyan sand boa's coloring gives it good camouflage when hiding in the sand. Its narrow head is well adapted for burrowing.

The sandfish can move quickly over sand, thanks to its powerful legs and smooth, streamlined body. See-through eyelid scales protect its eyes from sand grains.

Creatures of the Deep Ocean

Animals that live in the deep ocean must survive some of the toughest conditions on the planet, including crushing pressures, little oxygen, little food, no sunlight, and icy temperatures.

LIFE UNDER PRESSURE

In the deep ocean, thousands of feet below the surface, the weight of the water above creates extreme pressures. Creatures that live at such depths can have no open spaces inside their bodies, such as lungs or **swim bladders,** as they would be crushed by the pressure. Even so, some seals and whales can visit these great depths. For example, the Cuvier's beaked whale can dive to a depth of almost 10,000 feet (3,000 meters). These animals let the pressure collapse their lungs, and take most of the oxygen into their muscles.

Species that live their whole lives in the deep ocean have adapted over time to their high-pressure environment. They are very different from creatures that live at the surface. They have jellylike flesh with few bones. At such high pressures, even their cells must function differently.

The animals living at these depths include such **invertebrates** as sea cucumbers, crabs, worms, squid, and sponges. The only **vertebrates** that inhabit the deep ocean are fish. Most deep-sea fish are very small.

Animals of the deep ocean are very hard to study. Humans need extremely strong underwater vehicles to reach the depths where they live. A lower pressure environment is just as deadly to these creatures as a high-pressure environment is to other animals. When **zoologists** have tried to bring deep-sea animals to the surface, some of the creatures have exploded.

Blobfish

The blobfish is a deep-sea fish that lives at depths of 2,000 to 4,000 feet (600 to 1,200 meters), where pressure is 60 to 120 times greater than it is at sea level. Measuring up to 12 inches (30 centimeters) in length, its body has no skeleton and is made up of jellylike stuff which is lighter than water. This lets the fish float just above the ocean floor. The blobfish eats sea slugs and worms.

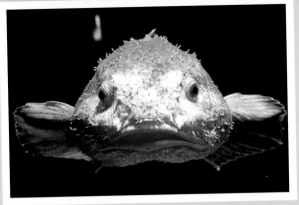

The blobfish has very few muscles and can only move slowly.

Sperm whales can dive to depths of more than 6,500 feet (2,000 meters) in search of prey, such as giant squid.

LACK OF LIGHT

It is dark in the deep ocean. Sunlight bright enough to support **photosynthesis** only reaches to a depth of about 330 feet (100 meters). Below that is an area of almost total darkness that includes most of the world's ocean waters.

Species that live in this environment have **evolved** ways of finding food and **mates** and avoiding **predators.** These animals have large eyes to sense what little light there is, sensitive feelers, and a strong smell sense. Many make their own light through a chemical process known as **bioluminescence.** The bioluminescence is created by **organs** called photophores.

Lanternfish are a group of small, deep-ocean fish. They have large eyes to collect as much light as possible. They are bioluminescent, using light to communicate, find mates, and attract **prey.** Their light also acts as a **camouflage** to protect them from predators. Their photophores are found mainly on the lower part of their bodies. The fish are hard to see from below because their glowing undersides match the light of the sunlit or moonlit sea surface. Also, the dark, unlit backs of many lanternfish match the darkness of the deep water, making them invisible to predators above.

The vampire squid lives at depths of around 2,000 to 6,500 feet (600 to 2,000 meters). To help find its way in this dim zone, it has very big eyes—the largest in the animal kingdom in proportion to its size. It may also use touch to find its prey, using two long, thin, **antenna**-like **appendages.** Unlike squid that live closer to the surface, the vampire squid does not squirt ink to help it escape from predators. Instead, it squirts a cloud of bioluminescent **mucus** from its arm tips. This confuses predators, giving the vampire squid a chance to swim away.

Bioluminescent bait

Anglerfish are found at different depths of the ocean, including very deep areas. They are so named because they "fish" for their prey using a spine on their back like a human angler uses a fishing rod. The spine is tipped with a fleshy "bait," which an anglerfish waves back and forth to lure its prey. For deep-ocean anglerfish, the bait is bioluminescent.

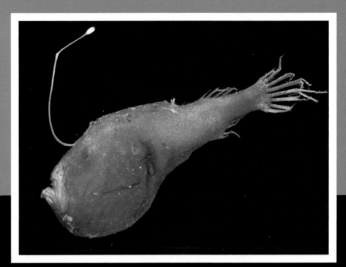

A triplewart seadevil is a deep-sea anglerfish that uses a bioluminescent lure to attract prey.

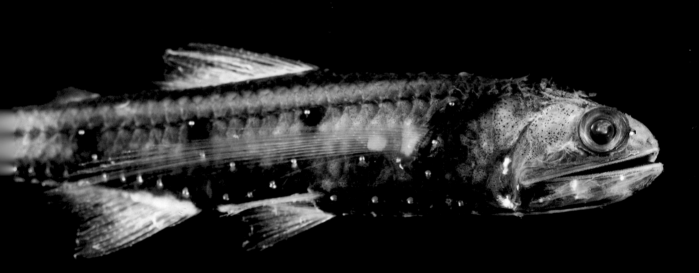

Most species of lanternfish spend their days in the deep ocean, but rise closer to the surface at night, following the daily migrations of the tiny living things that they eat.

LACK OF FOOD

With so little sunlight in the deep ocean, **photosynthesis** cannot take place there, so food is scarce. For this reason, deep-sea creatures usually have slower **metabolisms** than animals living closer to the surface, so they can go longer without a meal.

Deep-sea animals mostly eat **detritus** that sinks down from the upper ocean. When such large animals as whales, squid, and sharks die, their bodies are huge food sources for the creatures living on the ocean floor.

The sea cucumber is an **invertebrate** related to sea urchins and starfish. Sea cucumbers are found on sea floors all over the world, including in some of the deepest parts of the ocean. Their bodies are made of a tough, jellylike **tissue** that can survive the extreme pressures of the ocean floor. Many live their whole lives on the sea floor, while others float above it, and still others swim freely. They mainly eat detritus that floats down from the upper ocean. The sea cucumber's mouth is at one end of its body. It is surrounded by tentacles that catch food and pass it into the mouth.

PREDATORS

Some deep-sea creatures get their food by eating other animals that live in the depths. Most of these **predators** are weak and slow. Rather than chasing their **prey,** they prefer to ambush them, or lure them with **bioluminescence.**

Because so few animals live in the deep ocean, predators must be prepared to eat anything that comes their way, including animals that are the same size or larger than them. For this reason, deep-sea predators typically have long, sharp teeth, big jaws, and bodies that can swell up. Examples include bristlemouths, anglerfish, viperfish, barracudinas, daggertooths, and fangtooths.

The elongated bristlemouth fish is found in warm seas and oceans around the world.

Pelican eel

The pelican eel is a strange-looking deep-sea fish with an eel-like body and a huge mouth, much larger than its body. It may use its mouth like a net, swimming into clusters of small **crustaceans** with its mouth open and scooping them up along with lots of water. It then gets rid of the seawater through its gill slits.

The pelican eel has a hinged jaw that swings wide open for scooping up huge amounts of prey.

Hydrothermal Vents

All the deep-sea animals you read about on the previous pages somehow need energy from the sun. Tiny living things create **nutrients** near the surface of the ocean through **photosynthesis.** These living things and the animals that eat them in turn feed a large community of deep-sea animals when they die or travel down to the lower ocean.

But there are also many animals living in the deep ocean that do not need or use energy from the sun. These animals live instead on chemicals flowing out of hydrothermal (*hy druh THUR muhl*) vents. A hydrothermal vent is a crack in the ocean floor. Hot water gushes out of the vent. The water is heated by the same kind of activity that causes volcanoes. The ocean floor is part of Earth's crust. Boiling water breaks through the crust to form a vent. **Bacteria** use chemicals in this heated water to make organic material—a process called chemosynthesis (*KEE moh SIHN thuh sihs).*

The bacteria are the basis of an **ecosystem.** Small, simple **crustaceans** called amphipods and copepods eat the bacteria, and these crustaceans are, in turn, eaten by larger animals. Other animals keep the bacteria in their bodies and use as food what the bacteria give off. Scientists have found hundreds of new **species** living around hydrothermal vents, including snails, shrimp, crabs, clams, worms, and fish.

GIANT TUBEWORMS live near hydrothermal vents and can grow to around 5 feet (1.5 meters) long. They have no mouth or stomach and get all their nutrition from bacteria that live inside them. The tubeworm takes in chemicals, especially sulfur, from the vent waters. The bacteria inside it use the chemicals to make energy and food for the tubeworm.

Hydrothermal vents are certainly extreme environments. Temperatures and pressures are very high, and the vents spew out poisonous chemicals. The animals that live near such vents have developed different adaptations to cope with these conditions. One example is the Pompeii worm. The worm clings to the walls of "black smokers"—very hot vents that build tall tubes called chimneys. The worm survives temperatures of around 175 °F (80 °C) by growing a thick, protective layer of bacteria around it. The worm feeds the bacteria a sugary **mucus** given off from tiny **glands** in its back.

High Life

Animals that live at high elevations, such as mountaintops and high plateaus (*pla TOHZ*), can survive many challenging conditions. Such conditions include low oxygen levels, cold temperatures, intense sun, bad weather, scarce food, and dangerous terrain.

FOOD

At the tops of high mountains, there is less air, and there is little if any soil, making it hard for plants to grow. **Species** of animals that live on mountains have adapted to survive on the little food that exists in these environments. The tahr, a **species** of wild goat that lives in the Himalayas, eats almost any plants it can find, including grass, wild herbs, and leaves. Like many hoofed **mammals,** the tahr has a stomach with several sections. The different sections, combined with lots of chewing, allow the tahr to squeeze as many **nutrients** as it can from the tough grasses and stems.

The pika, a relative of the rabbit that lives in the mountains of Asia, gathers plants in the summer, then dries them in the sun and stores them to eat during winter. The ibex survives on moss, lichens, and tough grass, and even licks the rocks for the salt they contain. Mountain birds called wallcreepers have long, thin beaks for picking **insects** out of cracks in the rocks. Bearded vultures live by **scavenging** dead mountain animals. The Himalayan jumping spider lives at up to 22,000 feet (6,700 meters), higher than almost any animal on Earth. Its only source of food is insects that are blown up the mountainside from lower down.

Terrain

Animals that live on mountains are well adapted to the terrain. They are sure-footed and agile on the steep slopes and jagged rocks, and can move quickly when chasing **prey** or running away from **predators.** The ibex, a wild goat of the European Alps, has hooves with a hard outer edge and a soft inner pad. They give the ibex a strong grip when climbing, but also cushion its landings when it jumps between rocks.

The ibex is well adapted to its rocky, Alpine terrain.

A pika in the Canadian Rocky Mountains gathers food for the winter.

COLD TEMPERATURES

Mountains can be very cold places, especially during winter, and animals have found different ways to survive low temperatures and the snow and ice they bring. Some, such as the bighorn sheep of North America's Rocky Mountains, migrate to lower elevations during the cold months. This is called **altitudinal** (*al tuh TOO duh nuhl*) **migration.** Some smaller **mammals,** including the alpine marmot and the ground squirrel, find underground burrows and **hibernate** through the winter.

The yak is a mammal of the Himalayas that is related to the bison. It has no need to migrate or hibernate because it is adapted to cope with mountain winters, and can survive at temperatures as low as -40 °F (-40 °C). In proportion to the size of its body, the yak has a short neck, short limbs, small ears, and a short tail. This gives it a small surface area compared to its size, helping it keep in heat. For insulation, it has an outer coat of long hair and an undercoat of dense fur. A thick layer of fat beneath the skin further protects it from the cold.

The mountain stone weta, a large **insect** that lives at high altitudes on New Zealand's South Island, solves the problem of cold winters by letting itself freeze. During the winter months it goes into a state of hibernation, and 82 percent of its body's water freezes. As temperatures get colder, water leaves the weta's cells and freezes in the spaces in between them. Because the water does not freeze inside of the cells, they are not harmed. When spring arrives, the insect thaws out and becomes active again.

To deal with low temperatures, one **species** of alpine butterfly has dark wing colors. Dark colors hold more heat from the sun than pale colors, making the butterfly warmer. A study of the species *Colias nastes* (*COH lee ahs NAS teez),* which lives on North America's Rocky Mountains, showed that butterflies with darker wings were more active than lighter-colored ones. They also traveled greater distances and were less likely to be caught by **predators.**

Springtails

Springtails, a family of tiny, six-legged **invertebrates,** have an unusual way of coping with mountain winters. Their blood contains a substance that lowers the freezing point of their bodily fluids, so they can survive sub-freezing temperatures.

A springtail on snow. These animals stay active even in winter.

The yak's double coat keeps it warm during the Himalayan winters.

Snow Leopard

The snow leopard is a big cat that lives high up in the mountain ranges of central and southern Asia. It may climb to places up to 18,000 feet (5,500 meters) above sea level and is well adapted to life in the mountains. The snow leopard has a stocky bod, and small, rounded ears to limit heat loss, and its coat of long, dense fur helps keep out the cold. The leopard also has large nasal cavities (spaces in its head), which warm the air it breathes before the air reaches its lungs, protecting its insides from the cold. When it is resting, the snow leopard can keep itself warm by wrapping its long, thick tail around its body.

An adult snow leopard's 3-foot- (90-centimeter-) long tail helps it keep its balance on the steep, rocky mountain terrain. Balance and sure-footedness are extremely important in an environment of narrow ridges and steep cliffs. The snow leopard has long, powerful back legs so it can leap easily from rock to rock. The snow leopard can leap up to 50 feet (15 meters). It has wide paws that spread out its weight when walking on snow. The paws have thick, fur-covered pads on their undersides to help hold their grip on icy surfaces.

The SNOW LEOPARD has good senses of sight, smell, and hearing. This helps it when hunting for prey.

The snow leopard's large, muscular chest helps it to take deep breaths and draw as much oxygen as possible from the thin mountain air. This gives it the speed and endurance it needs to chase down its **prey.** Snow leopards mainly hunt wild sheep and goats, as well as birds and small **mammals.** A snow leopard's fur, which is smoky grey with dark spots, **camouflages** it well in its mountain **habitat,** so it can get close to its prey before pouncing.

Cave Dwellers

There are groups of animals that spend their entire lives underground in caves. These creatures survive in conditions of total darkness, high humidity, and little food. Vision (seeing), a necessary sense for other animals, is useless in a dark, underground world.

LIFE UNDERGROUND

Caves are useful places for many animals. Caves are warm in the winter, cool in the summer, and can keep animals living in them safe from **predators.** So many kinds of animals, such as bats, bears, birds, snakes, **insects,** and spiders, spend part of their lives in caves. But these animals must come out of caves to find food or **mates.** Such animals are called **trogloxenes** (*TRAWG luh seenz).* True cave dwellers—also known as **troglobites** (*TRAWG luh byts)*—are animals that live entirely in the dark parts of caves and cannot survive outside these environments.

Many different kinds of animal have adapted to life spent completely underground. They include **species** of insect, spider, centipede, worm, salamander, **crustacean,** and fish. There are over 7,700 known species of animals that live only in caves, but researchers think there are many more. This is because some 90 percent of caves do not have openings large enough for people to enter. Also, species that live in caves **evolve** alone. Because they cannot survive outside their cave environment, species cannot spread to other caves, so every cave could possibly have its own separate community of animals.

LIFE IN THE DARK

Troglobites live in a completely dark world. Because of this, most have bad vision or are totally blind. Instead, these animals have strong senses of touch, smell, and hearing to find their way. In a dark world, there is no need for coloring or **camouflage.** So the bodies of many cave dwellers have no **pigment,** and are pinkish, white, or see-through. Cave dwellers also often have long legs with feet adapted for moving across rocky, slippery surfaces.

Mexican tetra

The Mexican tetra is a fish that lives in the ponds and rivers of Mexico. Two forms of this species have developed—a normal form, and a blind cave form. The blind tetra has no eyes and finds its way through caves with **organs** that can feel pressure and movement in the water. But both eyed and eyeless forms belong to the same species and can breed with each other.

The blind Mexican tetra is adapted to life in underground rivers and lakes. It has no eyes or pigment.

Like many troglobites, this cave crayfish has long antennae and no eyes or pigment.

Olm

The olm, or proteus (*PROH tee uhs*), is a salamander found in the underground waters of caves in the central European countries of Slovenia and Croatia. The largest cave dweller found so far, it can measure as much as 1 foot (30 centimeters) in length. It has no **pigment** and is sometimes called the "human fish," due to its pale, pinkish skin. The olm eats other cave dwellers, including worms, aquatic **insects,** and snails. When food is scarce, the olm can slow its **metabolism.** It can go for up to ten years without eating. Fish and other **amphibians** are its main **predators.**

The olm is born with working eyes, but after four months the eyes stop growing and waste away, and are soon covered in skin. The olm is not completely blind, though, as it can still sense light. In the darkness of the cave, it must move around and hunt using other senses, especially hearing and smell. Its sensitive ears pick up vibrations in the water and through the ground. **Zoologists** think it may also be able to sense Earth's **magnetic field** and use this to find its way in the darkness.

Having **evolved** in the isolated environment of its caves for some 20 million years, the olm has developed some unusual traits. Unlike most amphibians, it spends its entire life in the water. To do so, adults keep some of the features they hatched with, including red, feathery gills. Most amphibians lose such features as they grow into adults.

The olm may have been the first **troglobite** ever seen by people. In the 1600's, heavy rains flooded a network of caves in Slovenia. A number of olms were washed to the surface. The people who found these small, pink, serpent-like creatures believed they were baby dragons. A local legend soon sprang up that great dragons lived beneath Earth's surface. To this day, many Slovenians refer to olms as baby dragons.

An OLM in a cave in Slovenia. The olm has an average lifespan of around 68 years, but can live to be over 100.

FINDING FOOD

There is usually little food in caves, and animals that live in caves must get **nutrients** wherever they can find them. They eat **bacteria** and other tiny living things in the cave waters, and prey on fellow cave creatures or **scavenge** their dead bodies, but most of their food comes from outside the cave.

Trogloxenes bring food in with them. **Rodents,** for example, bring seeds and nesting material. Such animals as raccoons and snakes often visit caves, and sometimes they die in them. Dead bodies are a feast for the animals living in these caves. Floods caused by heavy rainfall or snowmelt wash pieces of plants and animals into caves, which cave dwellers eat. Some **insects** and **crustaceans** eat tree roots poking through cracks in the cave roof.

In caves where bats **roost,** guano (bat feces) can form the basis of a small **ecosystem.** Few animals can feed directly on the guano, but bacteria and **fungi** living in the cave break it down into simple nutrients. Cave millipedes and small crustaceans take in these nutrients, as well as eat the fungi and bacteria themselves. Larger insects, such as beetles, eat the millipedes and crustaceans, which are in turn eaten by centipedes, spiders, fish, and salamanders.

In caves where bats roost, their feces are food for other animals living in the caves.

Kaua'i caves

In the Koloa district of the Hawaiian island of Kaua'i, there is a series of caves formed out of lava flows. The animal community living in these caves eats the woody roots of plants poking through the cave roofs, as well as on the waste of bats, birds, and rodents that come into the caves and **detritus** washed in from underground streams. The Kaua'i cave wolf spider, found in 1971, has been found in five of these caves. Unlike wolf spiders that live outside, which have eight eyes, the Kaua'i cave wolf spider has none. Instead, it uses touch, taste, and smell to sense its **prey.** The spider mainly hunts a single **species** of crustacean that also lives only in these caves, which eats roots and rotting plants.

The Kaua'i cave wolf spider moves slowly through the cave in its search for prey. Then it pounces, and kills its victim with a venomous bite.

The Hades centipede lives deep underground in caves 3,600 feet (1,100 meters) beneath Earth's surface—a record for a centipede. Well-adapted for life in the dark, it has long antennae and leg claws for feeling its way around.

A LONG LIFE

To survive for long periods without food, **troglobites** often need to have a very slow **metabolism.** The chemical processes that go on inside their bodies to give them energy and enable them to grow run much more slowly than for other animals. Because of this, they can live for a long time. For example, the lifespan of a crayfish—a type of **crustacean**—adapted to live in Shelta Cave in the southern U.S. state of Alabama can range from 19 to 50 years—much longer than crayfish that live on the surface. Studies of various **species** of cave fish show that they are generally smaller than their relatives living in outside water, but they live longer.

INTERNAL CLOCK

Cave animals may have slow metabolisms because they live by their own internal clocks. The metabolism of most surface animals is influenced by the day-night cycle. They may need more energy at dawn, for example, to prepare for a day of searching for food and avoiding **predators.** For cave dwellers living in total darkness there is no such need. Instead, they function on an internal clock. Studies of the Somalian cavefish show that its internal clock is much slower than the 24-hour day-night cycle, and can run for up to 47 hours. In another test, the Mexican tetra (see page 39) was found to use almost 30 percent less energy over a 24-hour period than its surface-dwelling counterpart.

The Somalian cavefish has lived for around two million years in dark caves and has lost its sense of sight.

Cave beetle

The cave beetle *Leptodirus hochenwartii (lehp toh DY ruhs hoh chehn WART ee y)* is highly adapted to its damp, underground environment and cannot survive anywhere else. It has many typical cave animal features, including long legs and **antennae,** and no eyes or **pigment.** Although this **insect** no longer has wings, it still has rounded, hardened wing cases. It stores moist air under its wing cases for breathing when it is in drier areas. The beetle, found in 1831 in a cave system in Slovenia, was the first animal to be recognized as a species adapted to a cave life.

The cave beetle *L. hochenwartii* eats dead bodies of cave animals and other detritus.

Glossary

abdomen the rear part of an arthropod's body. An arthropod is an animal with jointed legs and no backbone.

alga (plural algae) a simple living thing that can make its own food.

altitudinal migration migration between higher and lower altitudes, such as up and down a mountain.

amphibian a vertebrate with scaleless skin that usually lives part of its life in water and part on land.

antenna (plural antennae) a long, delicate sense organ, or feeler, found on the heads of various invertebrates, including insects.

appendage a part of an animal that sticks out.

bacterium (plural bacteria) a single-celled living thing. Some bacteria can cause disease.

bioluminescent describing a light given off by such living things as glowworms and deep-sea fish. Bioluminescence is caused by a chemical reaction involving a light-emitting pigment—coloring—inside the creature.

camouflage the natural coloring or form of an animal that enables it to blend into its surroundings, making it difficult to see.

cold-blooded describes an animal that has little control over its body temperature.

crustacean a group of mainly aquatic arthropods that includes crabs, lobsters, shrimps, and barnacles. An arthropod is an animal with jointed legs and no backbone.

detritus any collection of nonliving organic material.

drag the force that pushes against an object when it moves through air or water, slowing it down.

ecosystem a system made up of a group of living things and their physical environment, and the relationship between them.

estivate to spend hot, dry periods in an inactive state. Breathing, heart rate, and other body processes slow down.

evolve in a living thing, to change or develop over the course of many generations.

fungus (plural fungi) a living thing that usually grows on plants or on decaying matter. Yeast and mushrooms are fungi.

gland an organ in an animal's body that secretes (gives off) chemical substances for use in the body or for release into the surroundings.

global warming a worldwide rise in temperatures, caused by air pollution.

habitat the place where a living thing usually makes its home.

hibernate to spend the winter in a state like deep sleep. Breathing, heart rate, and other body processes slow down.

insect one of the major invertebrate groups. Insects have six legs and a three-part body.

invertebrate an animal without a backbone.

magnetic field a region around a magnetic material or a moving electric charge within which the force of magnetism acts.

mammal one of the major vertebrate animal groups. Mammals feed their offspring on milk produced by the mother and most have hair or fur.

mate the animal with which another animal partners in order to reproduce; the act of mating, when two animals come together to reproduce.

metabolism the chemical processes that happen within a living thing to keep it alive.

mucus A thick liquid that is produced in parts of animals' bodies.

Find Out More

nutrient a substance that is needed to keep a living thing alive and to help it grow.

organ a part of the body, made of similar cells and cell tissue, that performs a particular function.

photosynthesis the process by which plants and other living things make sugars from carbon dioxide and water using light and release oxygen as a byproduct.

pigment the natural coloring matter of animal tissue.

predator an animal that hunts, kills, and eats other animals.

prey an animal that is hunted, killed, and eaten by another.

rodent a mammal with front teeth made for gnawing hard things.

roost a place where a group of animals, particularly birds, regularly sleeps; the act of roosting.

scavenge to feed on the carcasses of dead animals.

species a group of living things that have certain permanent traits in common and are able to reproduce with each other.

swim bladder an organ in fish that helps them control the depth they float at in the water.

tissue the material of which living things are made.

troglobite an animal that lives its entire life in a cave.

trogloxene an animal that lives part of its life in a cave.

tundra a vast, flat, treeless region of the Arctic in which the surface soil is frozen all year round.

vertebrate an animal with a backbone.

zoologist a scientist who studies animals.

BOOKS

Extreme Habitats and Biomes (Savage Nature) by Angela Royston (Franklin Watts, 2016)

Fangtooth Fish (Freaky Fish) by Kristen Rajczak Nelson (Gareth Stevens, 2017)

Kings of the Desert (Animal Rulers) by Lisa J. Amstutz (Capstone, 2017)

Polar Lands (Life Cycles) by Sean Callery (Kingfisher, 2018)

Snow Leopards (Living Wild) by Melissa Gish (Creative Paperbacks, 2017)

WEBSITES

BBC Nature Wildlife – Animal and plant adaptations and behaviours
http://www.bbc.co.uk/nature/adaptations
In the section "Adapted to extremes," you can find information and video footage of animal adaptations to high altitudes, deserts, and polar regions.

BBC Nature Wildlife – Cave Dweller
http://www.bbc.co.uk/nature/adaptations/Troglobite
Check out these videos of cave-dwelling animals, like the Texas blind salamander and Thailand's cave angel fish.

National Geographic – Polar Bear
https://www.nationalgeographic.com/animals/mammals/p/polar-bear/
Learn how the polar bear survives in its Arctic habitat and the threats it faces. Contains information, photos, and videos.

Smithsonian National Museum of Natural History
http://ocean.si.edu/slideshow/deep-ocean-diversity-slideshow
Look at some amazing photographs of creatures that inhabit the deep ocean.

Index